And There Were 10!

JAN KELSEY

PAGE PUBLISHING, INC.
Conneaut Lake, PA

First originally published by Page Publishing 2021

Credit to: Tammy Lechner Photography
www.TammyLechnerphotography.com

ISBN 978-1-6624-5204-8 (pbk)
ISBN 978-1-6624-5205-5 (digital)

Printed in the United States of America

To All Women

This book is dedicated to all the beautiful smart wonderful women out there that have had negative self-defeating events happened to them in their lives. I promise you, you will find yourself in this book somewhere. What I want you to take away from this book is this: it doesn't matter how many times you fall down, it only matters how many times you pick yourself back up. My cup is always half full, even when someone else is trying to empty it. I encourage you to always stay optimistic and positive, even in the hardest of times. I have an old Irish saying hanging on my living room wall. It says: **Courage does not always roar. Sometimes, it is the quiet voice at the end of the day saying, "I will try again tomorrow."** So let me take your hand and walk you through my wild and crazy life. Here we go.

Prologue

What the hell happened? How did I get to the sweet (not ripe) age of sixty-three and have ten…count them…TEN… divorces under my belt? Hell, that's more than Elizabeth Taylor! I spent my life protecting that number. I never wanted anyone to know the truth because people judge, and I had been judged enough in this life so far. I literally could count on two hands how many people on this earth knew the truth, and four of those were my children. If you were married twice, it seemed okay; if you were married three or more times, eyebrows raised and opinions were formed. So if anyone asked me if I'd been married more than three times, I would very seriously look at them and very directly say, "If I tell you, I have to kill you. Do you really want to know?" The subject would get dropped.

But in my defense…NO ONE EVER goes to the altar with divorce in mind! Or at least I never did. I was just looking for that marriage filled with love, respect, trust, chemistry, longevity, and something that didn't look like my mother's marriage. Let me take you on my journey, but first, buckle up, this will be a wild ride!

Chapter 1

Now She Can Get a Divorce!

I had the absolute, most wonderful, sweetest daddy a girl could ever want. He had the bluest eyes, filled with warmth and love. Every deep blue-eyed man in the future would warm my heart, and sometimes, my bed. He came from a big family of seven, but only he and the four girls had red hair. My aunts were all very beautiful. Dad's oldest sister had deep-mahogany red hair, while the youngest sister had light-carrot red. The other two sisters fell somewhere in the middle. My dad's father, Pap Thomas, died when my dad was very young. I always thought that name was so cool. And as tradition unfolded, his brother would marry my dad's mother, Mary. Gramma Mary was short, round, had a full head of thick dark-brown wavy hair, a huge beautiful smile, and made the best cookies I can ever remember eating. I can still see her in my mind, even though I was a little girl of about five when we went to see her, in her small upstairs apartment in Kelso, Washington. I believe my father's loving, kind, thoughtful, sweet ways came straight from her.

My dad earned the nickname *Red* and *Buster* because of that red hair, or maybe because Reddick was his last name.

As an adult, I often wondered if he had to take a lot of harassment by fellow students about that name, especially since he had red hair too. My dad only finished the eighth grade so he could walk two miles to pick potatoes with his dad to support the family. Oh, but he was so smart. He would join the Navy in WWII, spend time on the USS Colorado, collect horrible images in his mind of men with legs blown off, receive a full set of dentures, and get out four years later.

My dad made a meager living as a carpenter. He built custom kitchen cabinets, as well as beautiful homes. But he was proudest of the fact that he helped build the seventh wonder of the world, Grand Coulee Dam. He used to make us laugh with his story of the guys putting a pair of boots, sole side showing in the cement wall, to make it look like a man was buried in the cement. I'm sure they got in a ton of trouble, but the story always made us laugh.

So about now, you're starting to wonder how this story and that book title go together. It will become clearer as we roll along, but first, let me introduce you to my mother!

My mother, Myra, was an extremely spoiled only child. She had the ultimate authoritarian mother and a daddy that she had wrapped around her little finger. She once told me that as a teenager, her mother would tell her she could not go out, but as soon as her mother left the room, her dad would give her the car keys. Her mother, Myrtle, died of a brain tumor when I was just nine months old. Don't you just love those really old names? Lynn Kay, my mother's father, would cause me hours of therapy as an adult, but more on him and that later.

My mom was very loving and very scary, all at the same time. When she wasn't beating my butt as I lay across her lap, with a rubber hose (age seven), she was chasing me with a knife (age eleven). I would tear out to the garage and hide behind my dad. He would stop the madness! The next day, she would present me with a new pair of shoes I had admired in the local Dennis Company window. This was a pattern. Be mean to the little girl, and the next day, when you were sober and the pills had worn off, be super sweet because you felt guilty. She didn't have me until she was thirty-six years old. We never had anything in common. She was a wonderful seamstress, made my clothes when I was little, cut patterns out of newspapers, and never taught me how to sew. She was an excellent cook, knew every spice, and just how to use them. She told me, her only daughter, to get out of the kitchen because she was too busy. To this day, salt and pepper are my go-to spices.

She was a hypochondriac, always complaining about some pain or ailment. She had pills for everything, and a doctor who delivered Tim and I, who lived on the other side of the state, would call in prescriptions based on their phone calls and her complaints. When you pulled out the top drawer of her nightstand, all you saw were white bottle caps. And they drank. My mom and dad were heavy smokers and drank beer. Hard liquor, mostly vodka, was saved for the holidays. I didn't know you could be an alcoholic if you just drank beer!

She was jealous of me too. She was blessed with a round body and little stick arms and legs. I took after my slender Irish father, and to this day, still weigh 135 pounds. When

I was in high school, she would get up and ask me what I weighed. Based on my answer, she would or wouldn't eat that day. When she wasn't doing that, she was telling me that the only reason she stayed married was because of us kids. My brother had already left home at seventeen, and now she said, "And when you leave, I'm getting a divorce so I can be happy." This one sentence would play a significant role in my decision to get married at sixteen years old. Words matter; be very careful what you say to your children.

By the time she was fifty-seven, she was peeing in ashtrays in the middle of the night, hiding her sandwiches in her pajama drawer, and almost burning down the house. She would put the corn on the stove on high and go sit down in the living room. My dad would smell the corn burning and run to turn off the stove. She would get up in the middle of the night and leave her burning cigarette in the ashtray, which was sitting on a little wicker laundry hamper with a pink fuzzy cover on top. My dad would wake up to the smell of smoke; thank God it didn't start the curtains above it on fire. But I didn't know that any of this was happening. It wasn't until I didn't get a little gift or a card on my birthday that November that alarm bells would start ringing. I called home, and my dad answered the phone. My dad never answered the phone. He finally told me what was going on. I convinced him to get help, but the government red tape was long, and it would be April of 1981 before she was admitted into Western State Hospital, a psychiatric hospital.

My dad and I went back to see her two weeks later with photo albums. We were shocked that she didn't know who we were. The attendant told us we had to get her wedding rings off because there were crazy people there who would cut her fingers off to get them. I can close my eyes and still see us sitting on the little green loveseat in the family day room. There was a cigarette machine there too, where the residents could roll their own and smoke, obviously a long time ago. The irony here was that once my mom was admitted there, she forgot she smoked, and never did smoke again. She had been a heavy smoker. Our minds are more fragile than we think.

I was twenty-three years old and now would have to play a game with my mother. I had a pretty little five-dollar junk ring on. I would pick up her left hand and say, "Oh, your ring is so beautiful. Do you want to see mine?" She would shake her head yes, so I would share my "very beautiful ring" with her, and then I would ask her if she wanted to trade. That is how she gave me her beautiful wedding ring. She had just passed her birthday in February and was fifty-eight years old. I still remember how paranoid I was the year when I turned fifty-seven. I just knew I was going to go crazy and not remember my family. Her life would end at the age of sixty-three, after not knowing who we were for five very long years. The first two years were spent in the insane asylum, and the last three were spent in a very sweet nursing home with a view of the ocean, close to my dad's house, so he could visit her daily.

One time I took Kelli, Casey, and my new baby, Penny, to see her at the nursing home. When I laid the baby in her lap, my mom began to scream and push the baby away. I think I know where that response came from. My brother and his wife had twins, a little girl, Katie, and a little boy, Timmy. My mom used to say how much little Timmy looked like her son Tim. And then at three months old, little Timmy died of SIDS. I think that was her tip-over moment. When we went to the funeral home to see him, my mom went up there and started arranging his little body in the casket because "he didn't lay like that." That really freaked me out.

They didn't diagnose Alzheimer's disease back then; they just said you went crazy or dove over the deep end or lost your marbles. They did tell us her drinking, abuse of prescription drugs, and intermittent malnutrition (remember when she wouldn't eat because she weighed more than me?) would combine to eat up brain cells that could never be replaced. I remember seeing in my mind a little Pac-man eating up brain cells. Oh so sad.

I want you to come away from each chapter with something positive you can apply to your life. So here goes for chapter one. All of us have things from our childhood in our closets, some more than others. I encourage you to dwell often on the positives, instead of the negatives. For me, that is my wonderful father. I can always close my eyes and see those big blue eyes and warm smile looking at me, as he called me "Sis." I can feel his arms around me, hugging me tight, making me feel loved and secure. Never let your past define your future!

Chapter 2

Beaver's Tail

Let me introduce you to my only brother, Tim. He was their perfect child. Tim was seven years older than me. He was super smart and talented. He had several diplomas by the time he graduated high school at seventeen, to include taxidermy and diesel mechanic. He used to make me hold the retractors while he dissected and skinned some of those animals. I was very young and found this disgusting and horrifying. Pretty ironic I would find my career as a surgical nurse much later. Oh, but that's chapters away. He was very artistic as well. I can't draw an apple, just saying. He was very mean to me. I have often said the only reason I was put here was so my brother had someone to pick on.

One morning before school, we were sitting at the breakfast table eating cold cereal, when he started using his spoon to flip milk at me. My mom heard my screams and came running in and yelled at me to go get cleaned up for school. Not a single word to him. Another time, we came home from school to find a note on the fridge, "Do not eat the pies in the fridge." So my brother did what ornery teenage boys do…he pulled the chocolate pie out of the fridge and ate all of it, but a couple of bites. He made me eat a bite, smeared some on my face, and then made me stand there holding the pie pan and the fork until mom got home. I got my ass beaten. Damn him. I have very, very thick naturally curly (frizzy) hair, the kind you can't do a thing with! One time, I had it pulled back in a low ponytail at the nape of my neck. In front of his fourteen-year-old friends, he made fun of me, saying my hair looked like a beaver's tail. I think I was seven. I've hated my hair ever since.

My dad was working on Washington State University Pullman College, so we lived in a small town nearby called Colfax. I have some very good memories of living on this farm. One of those was the summer my brother was running a combine cutting wheat, when he ran over a baby deer, cutting half of its front foot off. It wasn't very old and still had all of its spots. The baby took off running. By the time my brother caught it, he also came across the barbed-wire fence that the momma was strung up on by coyotes. So he brought this little fawn home. My parents took it to the vet to have the foot stitched up. Dressings had to be changed, and my socks were the perfect outside protectant. I don't think I had a pair of matching socks for quite some time.

Mitzey would run around our house on the hard-wood floors—*clippity clop, clippity clop*—such a funny little sound. I even found a picture of me kneeling with Mitzey, standing under one arm, while I held our puppy in the other. We soon had to move her outside to a pen. My mom would bring her warm oatmeal every morning. The Game and Wildlife Department said we had to release her back into the wild by fall. That didn't stop my mom from putting a pot of warm oatmeal behind the shed for her. We could always tell which deer was Mitzey, because when she was running with the herd, she had her funny little gait. On the day we moved away, she stood on the top of the hillside, with her twin fawns, to wish us farewell. But now, back to my crazy mean brother.

Age and maturity didn't change Tim either. When I was thirty-five, I had a party at my home to celebrate my new nursing job in the ER, and most of my new RN coworkers were there. I was still in awe of these nurses. Tim arrived with his new girlfriend that I had not met yet. They both were very drunk, but I remember thinking she had the bluest eyeshadow I have ever seen. I had stepped out of my blue-jean-and-T-shirt comfort zone to wear a silky purple-and-gold pants outfit. I was trying so hard to fit in with my new upper-class friends. When I opened the front door, there they stood, and he said in a loud voice, the kind the neighbors could hear, "Jeez, did you have to wear your pajamas?" My embarrassment knew no depths. Having self-esteem and personal love of self was never an option for me. He died one month before my sixty-third birthday. I didn't go to his funeral. I didn't shed one tear. I hadn't spoken to him in over twenty years.

My mom and dad did everything with Tim. All the camping, road trips, movies, anything and everything you do with your children when they're little. So, by the time they had me, they were tired of being parents. They didn't have time or energy for this little girl, Janis Kay. My mom said she named me Janis after Janis Paige, a movie actress in the 1950s, not Janis Joplin who was born in 1943. Another correction I would make often. I would spend my life spelling my name because everyone wanted to spell it *Janice*. My middle name came from my mother's father. I'm telling you all this so that later, when I change my name, it will all make sense.

As a young teenager, I was sat in the car with a bag of Doritos, a pack of Juicy Fruit gum and a Coke, while they sat in the Tavern and drank beer. Or I was given $5 and told to "go out with your friends, we trust you." They just were tired of parenting.

One New Year's Eve, when I was thirteen, I was raped by the brother of a friend. We had gone to his house for a New Year's Eve party. He had a little Korean wife that didn't speak English very well. I got drunk on screwdrivers, while they all smoked pot and drank. When the party broke up, we walked back to their house, just up the road. I was really cold, so I went upstairs to bed and turned the electric blanket on high. The next thing I knew, he was shaking me, telling me my blanket was too hot. I said, "Thank you," and rolled over. The next thing I knew, he was in bed with me naked. I did tell him no, but that didn't stop him. When it was over, I remember having my feelings hurt because he said, "You're not a virgin." Yes, I was, but all that masturbation by my grandfather when I was young apparently took my hymen. I felt ashamed that I wasn't a virgin, instead of being outraged that he had just raped me. I had no self-esteem, no power, no ability to withstand any confrontation, and no ability to stand up for myself. Such a mental number my mother, grandfather, and brother had done on my mind.

Chapter two comes with lots of trauma and heartache, perhaps like some of your chapters. But it also comes with strength and tenacity! No matter what other people do to you, stand tall, stand strong, and put one foot in front of the other! We got this!

Chapter 3

The Cowboy's Wife (No. 1)

When my boyfriend Daniel, that I was madly in love with, asked me to marry him, I gladly said, "Yes." I was sixteen years old, and he was eighteen. Finally, my mother could get a divorce and be happy. But I had to have my parent's permission because of my young age. We lived in Long Beach, and Daniel lived in Kelso, seventy-eight miles inland. I promised my father I would finish high school in Kelso, where we were going to live, if I could have his permission. I had just finished tenth grade and was taking my junior and senior year together. We were married in October of 1974.

As I had promised my dad, I went to Kelso High School's office the very next week to register. I was told those credits would not transfer, and they didn't have that same program that I would need to go to high school during the day and go to the community college at night. I said, "Forget that, I'll start my family." So I quit school and got married, breaking my dad's heart, and at the tender age of seventeen, I gave birth to my first child. Don't think for a minute there wasn't a lot of finger counting going on. Oh, and do you think my mother got a divorce? That would not only be NO, but HELL NO! I would forever hate her for that!

Daniel and I were so young when we got married and started our life together. We were young but so determined to have the perfect marriage and be the perfect parents. Probably because so many people said we couldn't. Daniel had a good job with Weyerhaeuser as a mechanic. We had our firstborn child, cutest little girl, just eleven months into our marriage. Twenty-three months later, her sweet brother would complete our perfect little family.

We were just kids ourselves. We used to play on the bed, and he would grab my big toes and ask me which one had the mole on it. I would always choose the wrong one, and we would laugh and laugh. Just for future reference, it's on my left toe, and yes, I had to look. We would go for motorcycle rides, and one time, a bee stung me right on the boob! Good thing I wasn't allergic to bees!

We bought five acres in the country, and his mother would buy the two-and-a-half acres across the street. We both had single-wide mobile homes and thought we had the world by the tail. Daniel's father had died in a tragic Jeep rollover accident when Kelli was only nine months old. He was a very nice, kind man. I was sad he wouldn't be a grandpa to my children. I loved having a mother again, but she was from another time, when women were told it was their "duty" to keep their husbands happy. Yes, you read between the lines perfectly. So any time Daniel and I had a fight, as most young married couples do, she was quick to remind me of what my role was. I guess that didn't sit very well with me.

In year four of our marriage, Daniel became disgruntled with his job at Weyerhaeuser. That summer, his mom would watch the kids so we could go on a motorcycle trip to Twin Falls, Idaho, to visit his uncle. It was while we were there, we picked up the local newspaper and found a "mechanic wanted" ad at Bell Brand Ranches in Wells, Nevada. We borrowed his uncle's Bronco and headed south to the six-thousand-acre ranch.

When you drove into the ranch, the cowboy's portion with cattle and horses greeted you. Six miles to the left was the farming side of the ranch, with all the combines and tractors. Six miles to the right was the main ranch, with the very fancy eight-bedroom house, owned by the California couple who had purchased the whole ranch just a few years earlier. That house was so fancy; every bedroom had its own color scheme and bathroom. I loved the lime green one the most. A very nice cook/housekeeper lived there full-time. I sure wished I had one. That part of the ranch was also where the mechanic's double-wide mobile home was. I can still see the orange shag carpet. I was ecstatic! It was twice the size of our trailer back home! Of course Daniel was hired, so we raced home to get our kids, truck, and belongings to move to this new adventure in our life. That decision would end up being the worst thing that could have ever happened to us.

We felt fortunate in our new environment to meet a young couple our age, Mike and Sally. They had a cute little blond four-year-old boy named Little Mike. Mike was one of the cowboys, so they lived down the road. We would share meals together, laugh, play cards—all the things couple friends do. I really liked Sally, and our friendship was strong. But I kept noticing Daniel and Sally looking at each other with "that look." We had moved there in August, and we went home for Christmas to Daniel's mothers. It was over a family dinner that I blurted out, "Daniel is having an affair with the cowboy's wife!" You can imagine the havoc that created. So we headed back home to Nevada. A very quiet ride, I might add. I convinced him to stop in Mt. Vernon, Oregon, so I could see my brother, his wife, and three kids. Once there, I announced to Daniel, that the kids and I would not be going any further, and that he could just go back to his precious Sally. Did I tell you she had perfect beautiful long blond hair? She was certainly more beautiful than I was. So there I was, single, with two kids—ages four and two. My marriage had only lasted a little over five years. And that is how I ended up with my FIRST divorce. Did the Ford light bulb just come on connecting the title of this book to my first divorce? Oh, you're so smart! Well, let's carry on!

Chapter three was my first marriage and the only marriage where I was left for another woman. If you have any men that left you for someone else, I want you to know this, it is their loss. And I can guarantee you that they have thought about us many times, with much regret, that they let us get away! Now repeat after me—dumbass!

Chapter 4

It Had to Be the Red Hair (No. 2)

I needed a job and quick. I went to the local tavern, the Wagon Wheel, and got my first bartending job. It was a good thing they only served wine and beer. My favorite tunes were on the jukebox, and I was having fun. I'd crank the music up when "Brown Eyed Girl" or "Crimson and Clover" came on. Did I tell you I have brown eyes? But there was this other male bartender, who was single and had blue eyes and red hair. Oh, that red-haired, blue-eyed thing. His name was Gary. The sparks flew, and the attraction was mutual. Gary had a very outgoing personality, much like mine. He liked to dance and have fun.

Gary's real job was as a logger, but in the winter, when it was too cold to saw down trees, he tended bar. He was from a large family of nine, half of them still lived in Oklahoma. But some of his families were local, so I finally had nice brothers- and sisters-in-laws. We were married in the little community church. I had a royal blue short-sleeved, knee-length dress that went nicely with his blue-flowered cowboy shirt and jeans. He told me he had never been married or had any children. Would I be willing to have children with him? In the meantime, Daniel never paid me any child support, but he did pay the $500 adoption fee for Gary to adopt our two children. Gary loved my children, and I was grateful all my children would have the same last name. (A little side note: Sally left Mike and Little Mike to be with Daniel. They got married and ultimately had two little girls together. But back to Gary.)

Life with Gary was hard. I learned a whole slew of new words, like eviction, disconnection, repossession—well you get the picture. We were dirt-poor. We moved back to Washington before Penny was born. And we would ultimately move back to Oregon before Tony was born twenty-one months later. Much later, in nursing school, the study of genetics would take on a whole new meaning.

Funny how the strangest stuff sticks in our memories. My memory from that time in Washington was a sturgeon (ugliest prehistoric fish you'll ever see) hanging from the rafter in the garage, and Gary skinning it like a rabbit. He'd then peel the entire side of meat away from the spine on both sides. We would invite friends over for fish-and-chips dinner. Half would be dipped in tempura batter and fried, while the other half was cubed and placed in boiling salt water for "poor man's lobster." It really was very tasty, especially if you dipped it in warm salted butter. It was a good thing Gary was a hunter and fisherman, or we would have starved to death, I'm sure. My father and brother were big hunters, and since I was raised on venison, this all seemed very normal.

When Penny was only seven months old, we were living on some land in Rose Valley, just outside of Kelso. We had lots of chickens and two calves. When it was time to butcher some chickens, Gary would chop their heads off, and Kelli and Casey would laugh and laugh as the headless chickens ran around the yard. It was all good fun until Kelli ran to the house, tripped, and fell on the concrete steps and chipped her front tooth. Oh, the good times!

We moved back to Mt. Vernon, Oregon, and Gary went back to work in the woods, falling trees. He would leave for the woods on Sunday night, maybe come in on Wednesday, and then go back out for the rest of the week. Tony was born, and now I was stuck at home with four children under the age of eight. Tony was just three months old. I was becoming lonely and depressed. This certainly wasn't the life I had envisioned.

I had a girlfriend named Laura to lean on and cry to. We all need one, right? One day, she said to me, "Get a babysitter. I want us to go out. There is someone I want you to meet." This sounded dangerous, but I was so miserable. I went anyway. She would introduce me to Jack, thirteen years older than me. He was so handsome, with his blond hair and blue eyes. He was slender, educated, and charming. He worked for the Forest Service Department and drank bourbon on the rocks. I thought he was so suave and debonair. He even owned two cars and a single-wide mobile home on a nice-fenced lot in town. Never would I have to be subjected to Gary's irresponsible ways again. So the next time Gary went to the woods, I moved into Jack's house, with my four children. Needless to say, that decision would lead to my SECOND divorce! My marriage to Gary lasted just long enough to experience Mt. Saint Helen's eruption in May 1980 and give birth to Penny in

August 1981 and Tony in May 1983. Maybe the hardest part of writing this book is keeping the timeline straight.

In this chapter, sadly enough, I did leave my husband for another man. Sometimes decisions are made based on the fact that we can't pay the rent by ourselves. Just remember, every marriage comes with good memories, as well as the bad. I've tried to include some good memories with each one, so you don't think I've spent my whole life in misery. Chin up, we never go to the altar with divorce in mind.

Chapter 5

Third Times a Charm (No. 3)

That's what was written on our quarter-sheet wedding cake, with white cream-cheese frosting, little pink roses with little green leaves. We got married in March 1984, in the judge's chamber at the courthouse in John Day, Oregon. We celebrated with some of Jack's close friends and coworkers. That is when I met Dell and Jan. Dell worked with Jack at the Forest Service in John Day, just seven miles up the road, and they would ride together to and from work. Dell would ultimately become a very dear friend of mine.

When Jack got home from work, I would be waiting at the door with bourbon on the rocks. Never did I think he was an alcoholic, he was just cool. But I did become intimidated by his college degree and my lack of even a high school diploma. I found out you could go to the local high school to take a GED test. They asked me if I wanted the two-inch thick book to study with. I had been a B student in high school, so I said, "No, thank you, I just want to take the test." Turned out I passed with one of the highest scores they had seen. I couldn't wait to go home and tell Jack. With bourbon in hand, I greeted him at the door, eager to share my accomplishment. He became angry. Not at all the response I thought I'd get. He said, "Are you just trying to show off? You'll never be as smart as me, you know!" I was devastated and, once again, made to feel worthless.

When Jack and I got together, he would bring me roses randomly and for no apparent reason. I would sprinkle pretty smelling fancy powder between our sheets. Soon, the roses would stop coming, and when I asked him why, he would say, "Because you're not worth a rose anymore!" Jack perfected the art of mental abuse.

From the beginning, it seemed nothing was going to be easy. Gary told me I had to give him custody of Tony and Penny, or he would take them to Oklahoma, where the other half of his family lived, and I would never see them again. I didn't have money for an attorney. I felt trapped, so I said yes, on the condition I could "babysit" them while he was in the woods. It felt strange to ask to babysit my own children.

Well, that worked for a couple of weeks. Now we were into September 1983, where the nights were dipping into the thirties. On a Wednesday, Gary called me to say he was going to start keeping them out at camp so his friend's girlfriend, who was pregnant with her first child, could have experience with kids, especially a baby. He would be there in a couple of hours to pick them up. Tony was three months old. Penny was two years old. I went into Momma-Bear-ballistic mode! I went into the closet, where I knew Jack kept his loaded service pistol, and I put it under a pillow on the couch.

When Gary arrived, I was ready! I didn't want to shoot him, just to scare him into leaving WITHOUT my children.

Remember, Gary wasn't really bright, so he charges me, a woman with a loaded pistol pointed at him. I threw my arm over the back of the couch and fired the gun intentionally through the floor of the trailer, thinking this will scare him away. Still he plunged forward. Jack flew into the fray, trying to get the gun away too, and after, a second shot was accidentally fired into the floor. I got scared and let go of the gun. Jack called the police, and because I was the one with the gun, I got arrested, put in handcuffs, and led out to the back seat of the cruiser, in front of Kelli and Casey—ages eight and six. This would be one of many times I would feel so bad for them.

Jack wouldn't pay my bail, but Dell would. My sentence was six months bench probation, only accountable to the judge. Years later, I would work as a paralegal for an attorney. He would get the entire thing expunged off my record. That is how I could enter the military eight years later.

The mental abuse from Jack didn't stop, and of course, I thought it would be better if we were married. Marriage was the answer to all problems, wasn't it? We got together the end of August and were married the following March. But nothing changed, it only got worse—surprise, surprise. He put me across his legs and spanked my naked butt, and when I would scream for him to stop, he would yell at me, "Kathy liked it a lot!" That was his first wife. Oh, the lies we tell ourselves.

Over Memorial Day weekend in May 1984, we would go camping with Dell and Jan at a park in Ontario, Oregon. We were in a tent, and they were in a class-A motorhome. One morning, Jack was being a jerk to me, as usual. Everyone was sitting around the fire, so I asked Jan if I could go into her RV. I just needed a break from Jack. She said yes. While I was sitting at the table, crying and feeling sorry for myself, I looked down and saw three full-prescription bottles in her purse. I didn't even look to see what was in them. I took them back to my tent, went inside, closed the flap, and started taking the pills by the handfuls, chasing them with beer. I would later think how weird that was because I had always had trouble swallowing even one pill. I figured if Gary had already taken two of my children, he might as well take the other two. Jack obviously didn't love me, so why was I even here. I then laid down to go to sleep and let all the pain and frustration just go away.

It was then that Jan opened the flap of the tent, stepped inside, and said, "Honey, Jack is an ass. You don't deserve to be treated that way." God does send angels when you need them the most. I pulled back the covers to show her the empty bottles. She screamed; they called 911, and the next thing I knew, I was pulled out of the tent, sat on the ground with legs spread, and Jack's finger crammed down my throat, trying to make me throw up. So I bit him! He slapped me hard across the face, and once again, Dell came to my rescue.

He said, "Jack, can I help?" Dell leaned down next to my ear and sweetly whispered, "Honey, don't bite me. I love you, and I'm just trying to help." I really wished Kelli and Casey were somewhere else and not watching this.

You know in the movies, the sound you hear when they shove a gurney into the back of the ambulance?

Thunk, thunk. Yᴜᴘ, I remember hearing that. The next thing I remember was opening my eyes to seeing a forest. I thought, *Where are they taking me?* As it turned out, the hallway of the hospital, on the way to the emergency room, had a forest mural on the wall. That was definitely somebody's dumb idea. Once in the trauma room, I heard people running around, someone talking to poison control, and someone asking me questions I couldn't answer. After I came around, I was sat up and asked if I wanted to drink the charcoal, or did I want them to put a tube down my throat to get it into my stomach. They needed it to absorb the rest of the pills I had taken. Little did I know that much later, in my early nursing career in the ER, I would say the exact same words one night to a very pretty little sixteen-year-old gal. Her boyfriend had dumped her, and she was heartbroken. She had overdosed on pills too. When I told her I knew what it tasted like because I had tried to commit suicide once too, she looked at me with shocked surprise and drank it as did I. Everything that happens in our life has a purpose. I will always believe my suicide attempt was so I could save a precious young life many years later. But it is true, if you've ever tried to commit suicide, you will think of this "out" whenever life feels totally unbearable down the road, and it would.

Later, Dell told me that Jack had stood in the hallway outside the emergency room and said, "She has embarrassed me for the last time." The next day, the doctor said I could go home, if I promised to see a counselor. I did, and the funny thing is, she said I didn't really want to die. I wanted Jack to rescue me and show me that he truly loved me. *Did anyone ever truly love me?*

By August, we separated, after he threw me up against the shower door in the bathroom. We were together less than twelve months. This would be my shortest marriage ever. I took Kelli and Casey and moved home to my dad, with my tail tucked between my legs. And so "three's a charm" didn't turn out to be so very charming after all!

Chapter five comes with significant pain and drama. More happened in this one year than in many of my marriages. The lesson here is that no matter what happens to you, God has a plan to use that, for your greater good and most likely someone else's too. I never think about my suicide attempt without thinking about the beautiful girl I helped to save. If that thought ever crosses your mind, I hope you find strength and courage from this book; sometimes just knowing you're not the only one to go through it brings comfort. Here is a quote for you to hang onto, "If you think you've blown God's plan for your life, rest in this. You, my beautiful friend, are not that powerful" (Emily Lark).

Chapter 6

The Pool Table (No. 4)

So, here I was, back at home in Long Beach, Washington, totally depressed. I had a little yellow house, walking distance from my dad's house. Gary would bring Tony and Penny to see me, ONCE, for a day. My guilt grew, and my heart broke for my little ones. I started spending lots of time at the Long Beach Tavern, playing pool, self-medicating with alcohol, and passing time. Daniel even came to visit. Sally had left him, taken their youngest daughter, and left him with the five-year-old little girl. We spent some time trying to get back together. I wanted it so bad for Kelli and Casey, but just like Humpty Dumpty, once broken, the pieces just don't fit.

And then one day, there he stood, long legs, tight jeans, bent over the pool table. Peter was blond, tall, slender, and had an athlete's body. He earned his living as a roofer. I thought he was so hot, and when he noticed me, fireworks went off! Depression be gone! We would start living together. The lovemaking was amazing, and I actually think I had a sexual addiction to him. Size matters...just saying!

We moved to Mountlake Terrace, near Seattle, for a couple of years. I had a really good job in downtown Seattle with Koehler, McFadden & Co, big real-estate developers. It was kinda fun to ride a bus to and from work, instead of fighting traffic and finding a place to park. It was a great way to get some reading done. Our offices took up the entire fifth floor of the Times Square building. That's the skinny triangle building at the end of the monorail. I was an accounting assistant. Who says you can't get a good job with just a GED? I watched them build the Westlake Mall from those big windows. One other thing happened while we were there. My friend Vicky, in John Day, Oregon, called me to say that Gary had been leaving the kids with this family while he went to the woods to work. The husband was in jail for beating Penny, and I needed to get an attorney and come get my kids. So I did. Life, going forward, would be forever changed based on that one decision.

What I got back was two little kids, five and three, with no manners, peed the bed at night, threw themselves on the floor with wild temper tantrums, and Tony had a very limited vocabulary. He didn't know what a train or an elephant was. I put Penny in kindergarten, and two weeks later, they called me to come get her; she was climbing on the desks and doing summersaults on the floor. No, she was not ready. Gary's parenting skills consisted of asking them to move because he couldn't see the television. God only knows what these two little kids saw and heard at such a tender age. Penny had been Tony's mother, fixing them toast and cereal in the mornings. She took him to the park, a few blocks away, by herself.

Gary had taken Tony when he was just three months old. Tony never bonded as a newborn. There's a whole baby chimpanzee study on the effects of not bonding. It's pretty sad, but it describes Tony perfectly. Tony would spend most of his life in and out of prison. I haven't heard from him since he got out two years ago. I guess he doesn't need a pen pal or money deposited on his account anymore. He certainly doesn't need a mother, or maybe he doesn't think he ever had one. I spent half my life dealing with the guilt I packed around for this child.

I felt so sorry for Kelli and Casey, so much attention was given in trying to control Tony and Penny; there was little attention left over for them. I had two really smart, good kids and two really naughty children, all from the same mother, raised with the same rules, the only difference was their fathers. I told you a lesson in genetics was coming.

Peter and I moved from Mount Lake Terrace to Kelso, where we would get married in May 1988. I would get a job at Wauna Paper Mill, and Tony would set the ottoman on fire. Tony and Penny continually brought chaos into our lives. Peter drank a lot, and we fought a lot. No surprise there.

My dad was diagnosed with end-stage lung cancer. He would come to live with us for a couple of weeks before he went to the nursing home. The nursing home was on my way home from work, so I would stop every day to see him. One day, at my visit, I noticed the light was burned out over his bed. It was dark and gloomy. I went to the nurse's station to complain and was told it was on the maintenance guys list of to-dos! I was furious! I went to the local furniture store, just a few blocks away. I came back with a sweet little coffee-table-living-room lamp, plugged it in, and gave my daddy light! Probably the one and only thing I could control. This was becoming so painful for me. My dad was such a good man. I believe God blessed him with minimal pain as his reward. I'm sure many more blessings were given to him when he reached heaven. He only took Tylenol for pain; he wouldn't do chemo, said too many of his friends did chemo and died anyway after puking their guts out. He just wasn't going to do it. I watched him just physically waste away over three months' time. I think he weighed eighty-five pounds when he died in March 1989. He outlived my mother by five years. I was thirty-two years old and both my parents were gone. I was in my fourth marriage, and now I was left feeling abandoned here on earth.

My escape was going to work at the paper mill every day. There, I felt important. I had twelve floor supervisors who came to see me at the end of every day to give me the production numbers off their machines. I made friends with one of them; his name was Randy. Randy was divorced and would complain about his girlfriend, who ran up his credit cards and just got up and left. I would complain about Peter's drinking and our fighting. We had great empathy and sympathy for each other. That friendship would deepen, an affair would begin, and a FOURTH marriage would end. Peter and I were together for five years. Years down the road, my sister-in-law from that marriage would contact me to tell me Peter had died of a brain aneurysm. He was a good man; this made me sad.

What I want you to take away from this chapter is that your education level does not define you or how smart you are. I was an accounting assistant for a large real estate developer—with a GED. Always sell yourself, with your big smile, your twinkling eyes, your fun personality, and your perseverance. If I can do it, you can too.

Chapter 7

I'll Find a Way to Pay for It (No. 5)

Randy and I moved into a large three-story farmhouse on the edge of Clatskanie, Oregon. The town was small and sweet. We both still worked at the local paper mill. It was then that I received $5,000 from my dad's life insurance policy. This was more money than I had ever had in my life. I paid for us to go to Hawaii and have an all-inclusive wedding, with matching Hawaiian coral-flowered full-length dress and matching shirt for him. I laughed when I bought coral-colored blush. My skin has pink tones, and that is all I ever bought. As for the money, a savings account would have been a better choice. Hindsight will always be twenty-twenty. But at the end of the week in paradise, we were back at home, back to work and back to the chaos.

It was then that I decided I needed a better-paying job. You see, more than half of Randy's checks went to his first wife for child support and alimony. I was so pissed off. If this marriage failed, I knew I couldn't support my four kids on what I made as a secretary. I couldn't even get child support out of Gary. Gary only worked for cash to pay his bar tab and not pay me child support. I even had him thrown in jail for nonpayment of child support. A few weeks later,

I was contacted by Oregon State. Would I agree with Gary getting out of jail to take an on-the-job training to be a diesel mechanic? I said "Sure, I only wanted some child support." After two weeks at this new job, Gary quit. I never saw a penny, and he never went back to jail. What a fool I am. Karma is a bitch though! Years later, Gary died of liver cirrhosis from drinking too much. I had no emotion about this one. If they die, do I still have to count them? Just asking…

In order to get a better-paying job, I had to get more education. So I went to the community college and talked to a guidance counselor. She asked me what I wanted to do? I said, "I had no clue." She sat me down to a computer to answer 240 questions, so the computer could spit out the top 20 jobs I'd be good at. The first one: a school teacher! Kids? Not only NO, but HELL NO! The second one: a ship's captain! I guess being organized and a little bossy might pay off after all. The third one: a nurse! I said, "Well hell, I've been nursing these four kids all this time, I can certainly do that!" So I worked full-time and went to school full-time, while raising four children. The first year was all the prerequisites. I'd have to get a tutor for algebra and chemistry, but I passed. The second year I made it to LPN (licensed practical nurse). Randy now said, "We can't afford for you to go any further. You'll have to stop at LPN." I said, "No, I didn't finish high school, and I'd be damned if I didn't finish this." I'd find a way to pay for it! It was May 1992.

You know those Army reserve commercials that say, "Just one weekend a month and two weeks a year, and we'll pay for your education?" Off to the recruiter's office,

I went. I was thirty-four years old. My first question was, "How old can you be to join the Army reserves?" When the recruiter said thirty-five, I said, "Then we damn well better hurry because my birthday is in November."

By June, I was in Fort Leonard Wood, Missouri, for three months of basic training. Yes, the same basic training the kids right out of high school go to. And it was Missouri. I was from Washington. I'd never experienced heat and humidity like that. I sweat from the time I woke up to the time I went to sleep. And it was the South. I was from the Northwest, where there was only one pretty African American girl in my whole school. Here, 80 percent of the 237 women in my company were Black! I wasn't prejudiced; it just felt really strange to be in the minority. I did learn a very important lesson in the Army. I don't care what color your skin is, I care if you brought your half of the tent and would cover me in a fox hole. Then there were the drill sergeants. Some of them were older than me, and some were younger than me. No one knew what to do with me. I would wake up every day wondering if they would respect me or break me. There are a million stories from my twenty-six-and-a-half years in the military. I'll save them for another book, perhaps.

At basic training, we only got to call home on Sundays, and only for a few minutes. Kelli would tell me she had to borrow milk from the neighbor because Randy wouldn't buy groceries. Randy would get on the phone and complain about the kids. I got to where I hated Sundays. September came, and I went home a new person. I had self-confidence, a very new thing for me. My family hated me. The rules had changed.

I spent one weekend a month at a Combat Support Hospital unit down the road in Vancouver, Washington. I could have driven back and forth each night, it really wasn't that far, but it was my escape from my marshmallow husband and my children, mostly Tony. I had met every policeman, fireman, school teacher, and principal in our town because of Tony. And then there was Randy. Randy would lie to me about anything. There's that lying thing again. Once he told me he quit smoking. I believed him until I found the cigarettes under the floor mat in the car. I was so pissed off and disgusted. It got easier and easier to take off my wedding ring as I drove out of the driveway for my drill weekend.

I hadn't been home from basic very long when one morning, Casey came down the stairs back-talking me. Typical teenage boy. I yelled at him to get on his face and give me push-ups. As he was pushing, he was saying, "Why do I have to do this?" Randy rounded the corner to say, "Because your mother said so!" Later that day, his wrestling coach would call me to thank me for what I'd done. He said kids needed more respect. I was busy that day too. Casey's room was a mess. Casey had often talked about going into the Navy like his grandpa when he got out of high school. So I trashed his room, Army style. Books off bookshelves, clothes out of the dresser, to go with all the clothes already strewn all over the floor from the closet. I even took all the linen off the bed and dumped the mattress on the floor. And then I put a note on the outside of the door that read:

"Dear Casey, since you don't like me telling you to clean your room, I thought I'd show you how the Navy will ask you. Love, Mom," and then I closed the door.

Casey had wrestling practice after school, so the other kids got home first. When they came in, I told them they could go look in Casey's room and read the note, close the door, and not tell Casey when he got home. I have to laugh when I think back on three kids and me lined up on the couch like little birds on a perch. Casey came home, walked past us, giving us a strange look, and went upstairs. I fully expected him to come running down the stairs screaming at me. Nope, he closed his door. We didn't see him for several hours, and when he did come down, all he said was, "My room is clean." I never had a problem with Casey keeping his room clean after that. Now, if I had tried that on any of the other three kids, they'd still be sitting in the corner crying. All children are different, raising them is hard!

After Kelli's high school graduation in 1993, we moved to Longview and bought our first house near the hospital, where I was working in the ER. One night, I was sitting on our bed, reading the newspaper, when I read that two young teens had set a car on fire a few blocks from our home. The window was down a couple of inches, so they filled the car with hairspray they had stolen from the grocery store, and set it on fire. The car was parked next to a boat with a full five-gallon gas can in the back of it. The back of the boat was parked up against the house, under the bathroom window, where the owner was taking a shower. Oh hell, this could have been a disaster. As I read on, my mother's intuition told me Tony was involved. I confronted him; he caved and admitted he was one of the two boys. I called the cops. Tony was sentenced to one year in a juvenile prison in Issaquah. Life just got more hectic. I worked two week-ends a month in the ER, drilled for the Army one weekend a month, and now one weekend a month, we would go to visit Tony at kiddy prison. I was exhausted and angry.

When this FIFTH marriage ended in June 1997, six-and-a-half years later, it would be the first time I didn't jump from one fry pan into another. I got my first apart-ment, had a good job at the hospital, even started going to church. It was a cute little Lutheran church not far from Kelli's house. I felt a connection there and decided to take the "Lutheran orientation class." It was in this class I would meet Jim.

The lesson I want you to get from this chapter is this… BE TENACIOUS! If you want something, be willing to do whatever it takes to get it. I wanted to be a nurse. I still am amazed at myself when I think about joining the Army at thirty-four years old. Don't let anyone or anything stop you from achieving your dreams.

Chapter 8

Dr. Jekyll and Mr. Hyde (No. 6)

What does it mean to be a Jekyll and Hyde? It means having a two-sided personality, one side of which is good and the other side is evil. This is how I would describe Jim a few short years later. Little did I know I would marry another one just like this later on that would devastate my life and my son Casey. But that story is chapters away. What a roller coaster! Hope you still have your seat belt on.

Jim was fifteen years older than me. He had a thirty-year career in IT at Weyerhaeuser. We started to date. He would send me huge bouquets of expensive flowers. He had a two-week vacation planned in Maui. The first week, his adult kids and grands would be there, but the second week, he'd be by himself. He asked me if I wanted to join him. *In Hawaii? Heck yes!* The week was full of laying in the sun, swimming in the ocean, shopping, fun, and great sex. He bought me a nine-hundred-dollar gold bracelet with Hawaiian flowers engraved on it. We also bought matching gold Hawaiian wedding bands. I'm still not sure how that happened, but we would get married in Hawaii, on the lawn, between the condo and the ocean. It was October 1997. Talk about spontaneous! We agreed to call each other's oldest daughters to tell them. When Jim talked to my Kelli, she responded with, "Congratulations, I'm so happy for you guys." When I would call his daughter, I got, "Let me speak to my dad!" And so it began.

Penny and Tony would continue to impact an already precarious marriage. Tony was in middle school, and Penny was in high school. Our home was a nice three-bedroom ranch, a couple of blocks from Lake Sacajawea in Longview, a beautiful man-made lake. When you came into our home, you entered on a long-tiled hallway. It was very slippery when it was wet. To the right was the laundry room and garage, and to the left was the rest of the house, but if you went forward, you would step down into a formal living room with light-blue carpet and a backdoor that led to an outdoor patio. One day, Tony came home from school wearing his Rollerblades rolled right through the house and out to the patio. The problem was he had rolled through some dark-blue paint on his way home from school, and now there were two beautiful navy-blue lines on that pretty light-blue carpet in the beautiful formal living room. I went into panic mode. Jim would kill us both. I called his daughter, who worked at a carpet store, and she came over with some special sauce, and we went to scrubbing. A good share of it was gone by the time Jim got home, but the wrath still ensued.

Penny had just gotten her driver's license. Jim let her drive the only extra car we had, his little bronze-colored sports car. It didn't take too long before she crunched the front left corner. More wrath. When Jim was being good to me, you couldn't ask for a better spouse. But when he was on a rampage, look out! I walked on egg shells, always trying to say and do the right things to keep him happy. He asked me to quit the Army, said I didn't need it, and the time away would interfere in our travel plans. I'm glad I didn't quit, but I did go down to a non-drilling reservist status. They only get fifteen points per year; you need fifty points to have a good retirement year. Because of Jim, I would have to make up three years at the end, but at least I didn't quit!

By the end of our first year, I moved the kids and me into an apartment to get away from his anger. That just made him angrier; he couldn't stand to lose. So he turned on the charm, courted me like a princess and wooed me back into the house. He even bought me some new boobs. I didn't want them because I had size A or less breasts, or because my first husband made fun of my "fried eggs" in front of our friends, no, I wanted them so my clothes would fit right. I have broad shoulders and strong arms, having a nice size C would balance me out, and it did.

Jim just couldn't stay Jekyll for very long. Hyde was always just one comment or action away from me or the kids. We even went to marriage counseling. But that only works if both parties are willing to take responsibility for their part and agree to change. Very difficult for a narcissist to do. I started looking for a way out, and not just across town. A friend of mine had bragged about a little cool town in Arizona called Lake Havasu City. Did Lake Havasu have a hospital? Did they need an OR nurse? The answer was yes. They flew Penny and I down there for an interview, and I was hired. Tony had already gone to Oregon to live with his dad. I packed up a U-Haul and Penny, and away we went.

I bought a house in Lake Havasu with pink rose-colored carpet; it spoke to my heart. This house came with a large pool and an aboveground hot tub with a gazebo in the backyard. I loved that house. I felt RICH. We should have been very happy there. I was so looking forward to a fresh new start. Six weeks later, Penny complained she missed her boyfriend back home. I didn't even know she had a boyfriend back home. She had started her senior year in Lake Havasu. I had even given her a great August birthday pool party when she had turned eighteen. Now she would use that, telling me she was eighteen, and I couldn't tell her she couldn't go back to Longview, so she did!

Finally, my tumultuous time of raising kids had come to an end. And so had my SIXTH marriage! This was my second marriage in Hawaii, guess that isn't paradise either. This hadn't been the motherhood journey I envisioned at seventeen when my first baby was born. It certainly hadn't been my happily ever after either. I had so much I regretted, and nothing I could fix. So I went to work every day to earn the money to play. Everybody else I worked with at the hospital did too. The weather was hotter than hell, but the lake was eighty-two degrees and crystal clear. One time, I was returning a video and left it in the front seat of my car while I worked. When I returned to the car, I found a puddle of black plastic. That cost me $68 because it was a new release. Murphy's Law! If you didn't own a boat, no worries, a coworker did. We all raced to the lake after work to have fun. I love the water and swimming. With boats come men, some single. Welcome to Daniel number 2!

Take this to the bank—you always have the power to change your situation. Be Bold, Be Brave, Be You.

Chapter 9

Naughty Nurse (No. 7)

Daniel was a big guy, and when he hugged you, you knew you'd been hugged. He had beautiful blue eyes. I told you there's something about blue eyes. Daniel and I moved from Lake Havasu back to Washington, just a short drive down the road from Longview and Kelli. Daniel started driving for Swift Trucking Co. It didn't take long for him to hate his job. I started working at the hospital in Vancouver, and I started drilling for the Army again. Daniel would pin on my Captain bars in 2002. We bought a house in Vancouver, near the Washington State University extension campus. I loved that cute little yellow house with the big-fenced backyard. We built a beautiful big deck on the back of the house and installed a six-person hot tub. The grandkids would come and treat it like a swimming pool. I would have bunco with three tables and twelve ladies on that big deck. I love outdoor living. We even put a bar on the back of the house, complete with neon palm-tree signs. Coming from Arizona, we decorated our home in all things Southwest. There were turquoise Kokopelli and sage brush-green palm trees everywhere—from the dishes, etched wine glasses, and twelve-inch wallpaper boarder in the dining room. I tell you this because down the road, when Daniel moves out, while I'm on active duty, he takes it all.

The Twin Towers were bombed on September 11, 2001. We were at war! It was January 2003 when our reserve Combat Support Hospital was called to active duty. We would spend two weeks training at Ft. Lewis, Washington, before heading to Turkey. But best laid plans gone awry again. Turkey's parliament had met and said the US couldn't play on their soil. Hmm. Okay, we will head to Northern Baghdad. Only, Baghdad wasn't safe for us to travel through. We'd have to wait. So our almost-three hundred soldiers strong reserve unit sat, in January, in old WWII barracks on North Fort. If you know Washington in the winter, it's gray, cold, and wet. Half of our company would come down with upper respiratory infections from the mold in the old heating ducts.

There was a General over at Madigan Army Hospital that had a Ford light bulb moment. He was so short-staffed, his operating rooms were down from fourteen to four. All his active duty nurses and techs had been pulled to the sandbox (Iraq), but there was a reserve Combat Support Hospital sitting over on North Fort, doing nothing. We started working at the hospital. We ramped up their operating rooms to fourteen, took care of all the retirees, received a General's coin, and I was happy to have something to do.

In the meantime, Daniel was home with the cat and the cute little apricot-colored Pomeranian named Phoebe, from *Friends*. He had gotten a job working for the city of Vancouver, driving the commuter bus from the park-and-ride in Vancouver to Portland twice a day, delivering all the commuters. It was part-time. Many of our fights had been about him not working full-time. I told him I didn't care what he made per hour. I cared that he put in forty hours a week like me. He tried to justify not working full-time because he remodeled portions of our house. I told him other men did that on their weekends, and maybe I shouldn't have to work full-time because I did all the cooking, laundry, and cleaning! He got a second job driving a limousine. He had to charge a three-hundred-dollar suit on his Bon Marche credit card so he could look the part. His first job was to take some high school seniors to prom and out to dinner. Teenagers don't tip. That was his only drive. I didn't want to be a sugar momma. Where was my knight in shining armor? Who would ever take care of me? I became bitter watching him drive for two hours in the morning, come home and lazy about till late afternoon when he'd go pick them up and drive another two hours.

Our reserve unit was sent home in May, having never stepped onto an airplane. But active duty pay was amazing. In 2005, our reserve commander addressed the nurses in formation. He asked us to volunteer to be nurse case managers. He explained that the active duty soldiers had a rear detachment that could take care of them when they came home injured, but the Reserve and National Guard soldiers had nothing. He said, "You might have a specialty like ICU or OR, but you're all 66H nurses." I had been a secretary before I was a nurse; surely I could do this. So I raised my hand and said, "I'll do it!" I would become a nurse case manager for the Wounded Warriors. There would be many more times over the next eleven years that I would raise my hand and say, "I'll do it!" At first it was called *Medhold*, for the Reserve and National Guard, but later, the active duty would join in because most of their units were in theater too. The name was changed to *Wounded Warrior Project*. My first duty station was Ft. Hood, Texas. My first year on active duty would take me to Ft. Hood, Texas; Ft. Sill, Oklahoma; and the last six months were spent at Ft. Riley, Kansas. I almost forgot. While I was at Ft. Sill for six weeks with my good friend Angie, I got a tattoo!

At that time, tattoos were illegal in Oklahoma. Angie and I wanted a tattoo to commemorate our active duty time since we were both reservists from the same unit. Our friends said, "Drive down to Wichita Falls, Texas…just a fifty-minute drive." On the way down there, we started to chicken out and decided to get our belly buttons pierced instead. I went first, not a big deal, and then Angie. While Angie was getting hers, I perused through the hanging poster boards that had all the tattoos on them. I found one of a sexy brunette nurse sitting on the floor. She was beautiful. Her hair was long and wavy; her dress was red and low-cut, showing beautiful breasts, but her nipples were covered. The way she was sitting, her short dress showed her little white panties. Totally sexy, but totally covered. Just like me.

We went back to the barracks, and for the next two weeks, I thought of nothing else but the pretty nurse's tattoo. That was it! I made a decision to go by myself and get that tattoo. I didn't want any of my friends to see what a big baby I was going to be with this pain. As it was, when

I was getting the tattoo, I had George Strait blaring in my headphones. Anything to distract my mind from the excruciating pain. I wondered how these kids could get tattoos everywhere. My friend said if I was going to get a tattoo, to go to this other place down there because it had a better reputation for cleanliness. I went back to the shop where I saw her, and she was gone. I was so disappointed. The shop keeper said, "Wait, I have some other ones from that same artist." I found one. She was blond; her arms and legs weren't quite right, but for $10, he gave me a photocopy. Off to the reputable shop I went.

When I entered, I asked if there was an artist there. I was going to need some revisions to my tattoo. I looked through books for the correct arms and legs, and for the next two hours, he drew my perfect sexy nurse.

I asked him, "Do you do writing, if I wanted something written under her?"

He said, "No, I can't, but if you write something, I can copy it." I love to write in cursive, so I wrote "**Naughty Nurse.**" My tattoo is about six inches tall, with my handwriting under her, placed strategically on the small of my back. I never liked the term tramp stamp. I preferred to think of it as "when a man was behind me, he would be making love to ME too!" I really did see her as me. Once in the locker room, another woman asked me if I was into women! I gasped and said, "No, why would you ask?" She said, "Why else would you get a woman tattooed on you?" Just too much to explain, so I just shrugged my shoulders and walked away. I've never regretted getting my tattoo.

If nothing else, it certainly has been a conversation piece. When I'm wearing shorts, her head peeks out over the top.

I finished that first one-year tour at Ft. Riley, Kansas. It was while I was in Kansas that me and Daniel's marriage would finally crumble. Maybe it was a curse to marry two Daniels! I just don't do lazy or lying! I was stuck in Kansas, while Daniel rented an apartment, got a full-time job (are you kidding me?), and took everything Southwest décor he could get his hands on. I was so angry. I took a leave to come home, painted the kitchen and family room a dusty purple, painted the living room, and half way up the dining room wall, in the deepest most beautiful RED! I had dark cherrywood sleigh-designed furniture with cream-colored brocade cushions. It was so stunning against those rich red walls. Later, when I sold the house, the first lady that came to see it, a retired school teacher from California, fell in love and bought it, offering full-asking price. I still think it was the red and purple.

I felt bad when this marriage ended. Papa Daniel had been a grandpa to my first grandbabies, two and four. This would be one marriage that hindsight would make me regret losing. Now what? Well, one thing was for sure, I didn't want to keep his last name, but I also didn't want to go back to my maiden name, Reddick. I wanted to drop the "is" and just be Jan. No more spelling it. I definitely was getting rid of the middle name Kay, from the grandfather who had shown himself to me and masturbated and fondled me from the young age of five. I would spend hours with a counselor at college to put all that trauma in the proper box in my mind. In that therapy, I also rescued that little girl, who was lying across my mother's legs, getting beaten with a fourteen-inch garden hose folded in half. She was only seven. Maybe I could finally start to heal.

I got Kelli and Casey together with me to make up a nice Irish last name. We searched the net; nothing sounded just right. Then Kelli said, "I've got it, Mom, take *Kel* from me and *sey* from Casey, and you've got Kelsey! I looked it up. It meant BRAVE! Well, I certainly had been that! On the divorce papers, where it says change the wife's name to _____, I wrote Jan Kelsey. It was October 14, 2005, when that divorce was final, and I was legally Jan Kelsey.

I encourage you to take on a mission bigger than yourself. Serving the Wounded Warriors will always be one of my biggest accomplishments and source of pride. And have courage to make big changes in your life. I had the courage to change my name to unpack that albatross. Remember every day… *Courage does not always roar. Sometimes it is the quiet voice at the end of the day saying, "I will try again tomorrow."*

Chapter 10

The Pseudo Cowboy (No. 8)

At the end of my first-year tour at Ft. Riley, the Army asked me if I wanted to extend for another year. I said, "Sure, but can I get closer to home?" They said they didn't have anything at Ft. Lewis, Washington, but they did have something at Ft. Carson, Colorado. Well, that was one state closer. I said yes. I had a black lab with me named Precious, who wasn't allowed to come into base housing. So I rented a ground-floor apartment and settled in for my second year on active duty. I never stayed out of the OR more than two years. I sure didn't want to lose my skillset. Life was good. I joined Match.com and started looking for someone to have dinner with. That is how I met Jay.

His profile said he was a retired Air Force Lieutenant Colonel. He loved western dance. Oh, how I love a good two-step! He was good looking, slender, with a nice smile. He worked full-time for Quest. At our first dinner, I would make a remark about having a nice LTC retirement check. This would be the first red flag. Too bad I never learned how to run when I saw them. He said, "Well, I didn't actually retire, I put in seventeen years and had a better offer out of the military." I remember thinking what idiot would throw up their hands as a LTC with seventeen years of service? But I gave him the benefit of the doubt.

A couple years down the road, we would be at his mother's house. I was looking at family pictures hanging on the wall, lined up the staircase. There he was as a young man, in military uniform, in front of an Air Force fighter jet. I commented to his mother, "Pretty neat Jay ended up a LTC in the Air Force." She said, "Oh no dear, Clay only did two years in the service." This was one of the many lies I would catch him in. His real name was Clay, but he had legally changed it to Jay. I guess that sounded better as a DJ. When we got married at A Little White Chapel in Las Vegas, I did not take his name, but of course, I paid for everything. This would be the second time I got married in Las Vegas. Turns out I'm not lucky either.

I loved Colorado with its 320 days of sunshine. I wanted to buy a home. In order to find something that would fit in my budget, I had to go an hour West and climb nine thousand feet. The town is Florissant. I would buy just under six acres with a double-wide mobile home on it. There was a small-fenced pasture with a loafing shed. It had a pretty grove of cottonwood trees with a little creek. I closed on that property February 6, 2006. I invited Jay to move on it with me.

It wasn't long before we had horses. I had owned a horse before. As I watched Jay struggle to saddle his horse, I realized wearing a cowboy hat and doing a good two-step did not make you a cowboy. He sure worked at playing the part though. His jeans were always perfectly pressed, and he could really dance. I liked that about him. We would work hard on this property, falling trees and stacking firewood. We didn't seem to mind the hour drive to work. In our spare time, he was the DJ for the local saddle club, and I rode my horse in the gymkhanas. It was a lot of fun, and we made a lot of friends belonging to the saddle club. I came off of active duty the following January. As a civilian, I started working in the OR at Memorial Hospital in Colorado Springs.

One weekend a month I drove to Aurora, by Denver, to do my Army drill. About this time, the Army decided reservists could not promote to Major without a bachelors of nursing degree. More school? Oh hell! The Army paid for it, and I started my degree at the University of Phoenix in Denver. It was a great program, each class was five-week long, weeks 1 and 5 were in the classroom, weeks 2, 3, and 4 were online. Eighteen months later, I graduated. Kelli and Matt would even come over from Longview, Washington, for my graduation. She never ever failed to support me.

My reserve unit's mission was to backfill Tripler Army Medical Center in Oahu, Hawaii. Seventeen of us were called up for a year deployment in November 2008. Sounds exciting right? No, it wasn't; it was lonely. My girlfriend and her husband, both nurses in my reserve unit, were there and loving it. When they were off shift at the hospital, they were island hopping and taking surfing lessons. I don't like to do things by myself (therein lies the reason I'm not good at being single…yet). I sat in my apartment drinking wine, eating popcorn, and watching a gecko run around, with my feet off the floor, I might add. To be fair, there were a few times I went to the North Shore and swam with the turtles.

Snorkeling sounded so fun, except all I could think of was water coming down that little tube and drowning me. So I floated on the water and looked at the turtles below. They really are majestic creatures.

My husband never once came to see me, even though I paid for all the bills, and he should have had plenty of money to do so. I even sent money home to build a beautiful new barn. When I came home at the end of my year tour, my husband was busy looking at porn on his laptop. Maybe not so bad until I found all the websites of guys doing guys! Let's just say, I had the sheriff escort Jay, the pseudo cowboy, off the ranch. That was after he ran around the house pulling down all of our pictures and putting them in the shredder. Oh hell, divorce number six!

I told myself I was tough, this was my property, and I could do it all! I would go get the four-by-eight-by-four bale of hay, have it loaded into the back of my truck with a forklift, come home and back up to a tree, hook up the come-a-long winch and drive out from under it. I got up in the dark to feed horses and dogs, and I came home in the dark after a long day at the hospital. I couldn't go out with friends after work; I had to drive the hour and five up the hill to get home to feed the animals. I loved my property with all my heart, but this was just becoming too much. I finally rented out the ranch and moved downtown into a cute little apartment on the second floor with a balcony. I met the lady on the opposite balcony; her name is Sherry, and we soon became fast friends. Her sweet pup, Gigette, would play with my cute little poodle, Tilly. We are still the best of friends, and she ended up being my maid of honor for husband number ten. Funny how life just goes round and round.

Lessons learned in chapter ten—stop discounting that funny feeling in your tummy when you think something isn't just right. Some say, it's your angel or the Holy Spirit trying hard to guide you. Some say, that's what you feel when a red flag pops up. Any way you look at it, STOP dead in your tracks and change direction. Because if you don't, it never ends well. Let us always strive for a life with NO red flags!

Chapter 11

Texas, Here I Come (No. 9)

I stayed in that apartment for almost a year. I bought new dishes that were red and black. I decorated the apartment all modern and cool. I even dated a guy named Dick that I had worked with in the operating room at Memorial Hospital in the Springs. He was on the heart team, and when I would see him in the hallway, those blue eyes would look right through me. Oh such chemistry. We dated for several months, but it just wasn't the right time. I became lonely and depressed. I just wanted to go home.

I looked online, and the hospital in Longview, Washington, where I had started my nursing career, had an operating room RN opening. I went online and found a beautiful apartment overlooking the Cowlitz River in Kelso, and home I went. Besides, Kelli, Matt, and my two grandkids lived in Longview. I'd have plenty to do with my grandkids and Kelli. But that isn't what happened.

First, by the time I got home, the job opening was closed. Second, Kelli was very busy with their electrical business and didn't have time to entertain me. The grandkids, well, they didn't know me, and my granddaughter wouldn't even spend the night at my house. I called up my old friend at Cross Country Travel and took a twelve-week nursing assignment in Olympia at St. Peters Hospital. They rented me an apartment there, and I would come home to Kelso on the weekends. For entertainment, I would go back on Match.com, only I had to move my location to the Olympia/Tacoma area. When I did that, Sam then saw my profile. He lived in Gig Harbor, Washington.

We met at an Olive Garden in Olympia for our first date. After hearing about Jay lying about being a retired LTC, he proceeded to pull out his wallet, showed me his Air Force Captain retirement card, his master's degree card, and anything else he thought would legitimize him. SOLD! During the next twelve weeks, he would come down to my apartment, or I would go up to his apartment in Gig Harbor. At the end of the twelve weeks, we bought a four-bedroom house together in a new development in Gig Harbor, behind a Target and Starbucks. Close by was the prison where he worked as an investigator. That investigator would come out in every argument we had. He would turn the tables and ask me questions instead of answering mine. I remember getting Botox in my forehead so he couldn't read my face and see what I was thinking when we fought.

I took a civilian job in the operating room at Madigan Army Hospital in Tacoma. I loved working there because I had already worked there on active duty and drill weekends, and it felt like home. I transferred to a reserve Army hospital unit that drilled at Madigan. Sam's parents lived in Austin, Texas. They were elderly, and we would call them every Sunday faithfully.

One of the funniest memories in that house in Gig Harbor was one Thanksgiving. Kelli, Matt, and the kids came up from Longview for dinner. Kelli and I had a great time, drinking wine, preparing our big dinner. As we started eating, my sweet grandson starting laughing.

I said, "What's so funny?"

He said, "Gramma, you stuck your boob in your gravy!" Out of the mouths of babes!

That spring, I paid for Sam, and I to go on a cruise, my first and only cruise so far. First stop, Roatan, Honduras. Here, we would tackle zip-lining. I was scared to death! It wasn't jumping off the platform for the takeoff, but the landing that mortified me. Somehow, flying into a big tree at 60 mph was scary as hell! But I did it! I was so proud of myself until the guide said we had twelve more zip lines to get back to the van. Oh hell!

Next stop, Belize! Sam had studied archeology in college, and he wanted to see the ruins. The cruise ship can't dock in Belize; you have to take a shuttle boat into the dock. From there, we got in a van for an hour-long ride on a bumpy dirt road and now would get in a boat to go upriver thirty minutes to the ruins. Ugh! What I won't do to please someone!

Next stop was Cozumel, Mexico. It was at the shops at Cozumel that I bought myself some pretty little Tanzanite earrings, and he bought me a one-carat diamond wedding ring. I had purchased our wedding rings in Gig Harbor (call me a sucker), so maybe it was time for him to step up to the plate.

The one thing that was never equal was our sex life. I wanted it at least weekly and preferably more than that. He was happy with once every six weeks. When we did make love, it was really good. During that "romantic" eight-day cruise, we only made love ONCE! I just couldn't figure it out. This wouldn't be the last time I would pay for everything, provide free healthcare through the military, stay fit and trim, have an active sex drive, and NOT be desired by my husband. After my tenth marriage, my son would tell me I was just too much! Men just couldn't figure out how to be married to me. I took it as a compliment. Their loss! My thinking, *If I'm too much, maybe you're not enough!*

When I needed a relief valve, I could always count on the Army to need a nurse. I volunteered to go on active duty at Ft. Sam Houston, San Antonio, Texas, for sixteen months. I drove the class-A RV, and Sam drove my car to a sweet KOA campground with a swimming pool in San Antonio in April 2015. He then went back home to our house in Gig Harbor. This mission was two-fold. I was almost ready to retire, and I would accumulate more retirement points, increasing my retirement pay, and I would get to spend more time getting to know his parents and two sisters in Austin. The goal was to finish my active duty tour and come back home to Gig Harbor. It didn't take long before I called Sam and told him his dad was "circling the drain," a nursing term for dying, and he needed to get down there. By June, we had sold our Gig Harbor home and purchased a sweet little house with a fenced backyard on Stonehaven in New Braunfels, Texas, which is halfway between Austin and San Antonio. The RV was now safely put away in storage. In September, Sam pinned on my Lieutenant Colonel black maple leaf. Wow! Who knew a high school dropout could make it this far? Never underestimate your capabilities. By November, his dad passed away. It definitely was the right decision at the time, even though his family would never thank me for bringing Sam to Texas to spend this time with his father.

And then I had a great idea to put the RV in Landa RV Park, right next to the famous Guadalupe River. I sold Rodan + Fields skincare and thought this would be a great way to have parties at the RV and have wine dates with my girlfriends. I also thought the RV would be a great getaway for Sam and me. Maybe something romantic? But that's not what happened either. On September 11, 2018, Sam and I had a fight, and he told me to just go to the RV. I said, "Don't ask me twice!" I grabbed my purse and my six-pound poodle and off I went. He never did ask me to return home. And so, I filed for divorce number NINE. Much later, he told me he thought I was going to call him and ask him if I could come back. I sure wish Mars and Venus could communicate. I gave him the house and everything in it, and I took the RV.

Here we go! Pride is a hard thing to swallow when you think you're right. Was Sam a narcissist? Absolutely! But I gave up my marriage, my home, all my beautiful furniture, my beautiful Doodles so I could sit in my RV with my six-pound Poodle and be right? I should have asked to come back. This marriage was worth saving, but I was stubborn. Was he stubborn too? Of course, but I could have taken the high road. Lesson: Don't let your pride and stubbornness dictate your path forward. Sometimes it is OKAY to humble yourself and let them be right. Take time to see the bigger picture before making rash decisions.

Chapter 12

The Best Love Story (No. 10)

Life was okay living in the RV. I was still working two days a week at the local surgery center, going to my favorite hangout, Water2Wine, dating a few guys off Match.com out of boredom, but nothing to write home about. Besides, who would I write home to? In December, Kelli paid for me to move into a nicer park at the south end of New Braunfels. In the meantime, Dick from Colorado contacted me again. We had always stayed friends on Facebook, commenting on our grandkids and such. He wanted to come down to see me for Christmas. I said, "sure," and then I called him the next day to say, "No, I'm not ready." I told him I had a camping trip planned at the end of February with some friends of mine, and he could join me then.

January came around, and on the ninth, Dick said, "Will you be home tomorrow? Something is coming for you."

"I'm just going to Pilates and then home," I said.

The next day, I was standing in my RV in my Pilates clothes, on the phone with my girlfriend, when I saw the white car pulled up in front of my RV. I told my girlfriend, "I have to go. I think Dick is sending me flowers from

Colorado." I ran outside, and Dick stepped out of the car, with flowers, chocolate, and a cowboy hat. What's a girl to do? We hadn't seen each other face-to-face for eight years. All of a sudden, I felt like my knight in shining armor had arrived—white horse, white car—same, same.

He came in, and we started to have small talk, and then I stopped talking and asked him why he was here. His answer, "I let you get away once, and when I saw you had started dating, I figured I'd better get down here and see if we still had a connection." My heart melted. Isn't that what every woman wants to hear? No one had ever driven fourteen hours, unannounced, to woo me! He spent nine days with me, in 310 square feet. If you can live in that small of a space, you will know if you're compatible, I reasoned. At the end of nine days, he drove back to Colorado. Then on February 5, he flew back to San Antonio, where I was standing at the bottom of the escalator in the airport, anxiously awaiting his arrival—with my short skirt, sexy blouse, high heels, and rose-colored glasses, firmly planted on my nose.

In February, we went camping with some good friends in Kerrville. The nighttime temperature fell below freezing point. Dick got up several times during the night to check the water hoses and ultimately came down with bronchitis. He slept with a CPAP machine, which made less noise than I thought it would, until he would turn on his side and break the seal. Then it was *whoosh, whoosh* with cold air blowing on me. I'm a light sleeper, enough said. And then came the night that his coughing brought on a seizure. He sat up on the edge of the bed, started coughing, and fell back across my legs, having a seizure. It didn't last long, but it scared the hell out of me. Oh, but this wouldn't be the last time. The next month would be hell. He fell down in the parking lot, he spilled red wine on my girlfriend's white dress, he dropped a full glass of beer at the bar—all because his coughing brought on seizures. The doctor told him he was prediabetic with his obesity, hypertension, high-risk heart attack, and high-risk stroke. At the time, I thought, *What the hell have I gotten myself into?*

I started keeping a written journal. When I didn't have my journal, I'd write in the notes section of my phone. Kind of a free therapy place where I could vent. Here was my first phone entry sometime before April 2019, when I started dating my entries:

> I'm angry at myself for falling for him so hard and bragging to the world about our love story and happiness. Boy, I'm the poster child for putting on rose-colored glasses. Now if we break up, I'll really have egg on my face. How embarrassing this will be.

On April 1, we took the RV to Galveston. It was pretty windy and rainy, so we didn't go out much. Dick was still coughing, but much better, no more seizures. My son, Casey, came to visit for a week. He was going through a divorce and needed to just get away. His wife had kept him out of my life for thirteen years. I was so happy to see him. Dick and Casey got along great. At the end of the week, we took Casey to Houston to fly back to Idaho. We stopped at Costco on the way back to the RV to try on wedding rings. Oh my! We moved the RV to South Padre Island for the last half of April.

While we were there, we ran into some of my New Braunfels friends. We went to dinner with them at Pier 19, a sweet little restaurant at the end of the KOA park we were staying in. While we waited to be seated, I was admiring a beautiful cabinet of turquoise jewelry. I found a sweet little ring and bought it. Later, Dick overheard me telling Linda the ring only cost me $28. He said, "Well, if I'd known it was going to be that cheap, I would have bought it for you." This would be my first glimpse of his penny-pinching ways, but no worries, my rose-colored glasses were still securely in place.

From the beach, we would be homeward bound, but first, we had to stop for a week in Lincoln, Nebraska, for a Kenny Chesney concert. Dick was a concert nut, and we had so much fun. While we were there, we went to the zoo and rode the little train like kids. We arrived at his home in Colorado Springs on May 20. On May 21, we awoke to fourteen inches of snow. It looked pretty strange to see snow on top of my stand-up paddle board that was secured on top of my two-wheel drive GMC Yukon. Hey, who buys four-wheel drive vehicles in Texas?

Dick had owned this two-and-a-half acre with a five-bedroom house for the last thirty-five years. It was the same house we had dated in eight years prior. Dick had been single for thirteen years before me, and it was so evident. Every room in the house, the garage, the barn—all looked like a man's cave with a hoarder living there, full to the brim. His ex-wife's clothes and wedding dress still hung in the office closet. Oh hell no! I had a tall job. I started painting walls on day 4. Before it was over, there would be four dumpster loads removed from this property.

There were large garbage bags of pop cans and beer cans. Cans all over everywhere. Why? Turns out, when Alan was in Boy Scouts, they collected cans for some project or another. Problem was, they didn't stop collecting cans, ever! One time, Dick was away for the weekend to go to a concert in Denver with his buddies. This was my opportunity to get rid of stuff. I collected cans until my Yukon was full to the brim, with seats down. Then I took them to the aluminum recycling place. Do you know how much money I got for all my effort? $17! Yup, it was easier to just keep collecting them than to get rid of the mess. I continued to shake my head over such laziness.

We found a wedding ring I fell in love with online at Costco. It had three beautiful square princess-cut diamonds, one carat center with two half carat diamonds on the sides. It had a bold simple platinum setting. It was $6,900. We looked at lots of rings. I told him I didn't like the ones with tiny little diamonds surrounding the diamond. Are you wondering if he bought me the ring I was in love with? No, he didn't; he talked me into a $4,900 ring with smaller diamonds, emerald cut, which isn't as sparkly, and lots of "tiny little diamonds" going down both sides. It always was about money with him. Later, in a fight, he would say, "I wish I had only spent $2,500 on your ring." Trust me, I'm worth a fifty-thousand-dollar ring, you dumbass!

June 12 was a Wednesday. Dick said, "Let's go for a ride." I was wearing my usual blue jeans and a T-shirt. He said, "You might want to dress up a little more." So I put on a pair of yellow corduroy shorts with a sweet Mexican-looking off-the-shoulder blouse, with lots of bright-colored flowers. I really did look cute! He took me to the Garden of the Gods, a well-known landmark in Colorado Springs. There is a huge rock there, balancing on about two square feet maximum. It is appropriately called *Balanced Rock*. We parked the car and started walking. When we got to the rock, he asked these two young ladies if they'd take our picture since he intended to ask me to marry him. More of my fairy tale was coming true. He got down on one knee and said, "Jan Kelsey, you balance my life, will you please marry me on Friday?" I did say it was Wednesday, right? This was the most romantic proposal I had ever received. Of course I said yes to my Romeo! We then went down to Manitou Springs to celebrate. Before we left, we drove around and saw the beautiful city park gazebo. That would be a cool place to get married, we decided. Our intent was to get married at the courthouse, but when he told his kids and grandchildren we were engaged to get married, the two little girls said, "Papa, can we be your flower girls?" How do you say no to that? So the race was on.

Thursday was full! First call was to the florist; yes they could do a red-roses bouquet, boutonnieres, and a bag of rose pedals for the flower girls. I remember pulling up to Macy's and asking God to help me find a wedding dress. When I walked through the door, it was the first dress I looked at, knee length, white—with brocade designs—sleeveless, and so beautiful. It fit perfectly. I added some pretty white heels and some J'adore Eau de Perfume, and I looked like the perfect bride. Lunch was spent with my maid of honor, Sherry (remember, she was my balcony girlfriend?) at the famous Jake and Telly's Greek Taverna in Manitou Springs. Still is one of my favorite restaurants. Now I was off to Michael's. I had to make rose-petal baskets for my flower girls. Remember, I'm the girl who doesn't have an artistic bone one. But I found the cutest little wicker baskets, some red ribbon, some yellow silk daisies, and a glue gun. How hard could this be? I did it, and they were kinda cute, if I do say so myself.

Thursday, Dick also brought me a prenup to sign. "Are you kidding me? The day before we get married?"

He said, "Well, it's a ten-forty rule. You're on marriage number ten, and you're over forty." It stated if we got a divorce before five years, I would get nothing. If he died before those five years were up, I would get one third, his sons, the other two thirds. He didn't trust me; he even said he wouldn't tell me what monies and assets he had until we had been married five years. What an idiot; didn't he know that all assets obtained prior to the marriage remained yours in a divorce?

Oh, but I would put his name on my savings and checking account. I would let him move all his vehicles and house insurances to my USAA, which meant the payment came out of my checking account. And of course, I was happy I could add him to my Tricare health insurance. He had told me he had spent over $900 a month on insurances and medications. Now he would only spend $80 every three months on meds. He also told me he was spending over $500 a month to Safeco for the car and house insurances, that he now paid $200 a month. It stung when we had a fight, and he said he didn't mind that I didn't come with any assets or money. The hell I didn't! Oh, but I guess if you don't have a fat 401K and own a house, you don't have assets. I brought home almost as much as he did every month, but I guess that didn't count either. This wouldn't be the first time I would think he had been single too long. I reminded him I had given far more away than I had ever received in my previous divorces. But who cared? We were going to be married forever! I took a deep breath and signed it. Yes, my rose-colored glasses were still firmly on my nose.

The wedding took place the next afternoon, the fourteenth of June, at that beautiful gazebo we had found across from the city park in Manitou Springs. Sherry's husband, Stan, walked me down the aisle—well, across the gazebo anyway. Dick's twenty-eight-year-old son, Alan, who lived in the basement, was his best man. Dick's daughter-in-law wanted to try out her new fancy camera so she took all the pictures, and you'd never guess we hadn't hired a professional photographer. All the pictures turned out so beautiful. Dick's hippie friend was our officiant. The ceremony didn't take very long, and off to the famed "Cliff House Hotel" in Manitou Springs we went. The Cliff House is very old, historic, and beautiful. We had a beautiful dinner with filet mignons, bubbly champagne, and crème brûlée for desert. One of his friends had upgraded our suite to a larger one on the third floor as a wedding gift. It was lovely with a view of the mountains and the quaint little town of Manitou Springs.

It was during dinner that the marriage license was passed around for the wedding party to sign. I had told Dick many times that I would not be taking his last name because of the headache of changing my name on everything. There was my social security card, driver's license, car registration, passport, every credit card, and so much more. If you have ever changed your name, you know how much hassle it is. I was the last one to sign, and in the blink of an eye, I found myself signing with the addition of his last name after mine. When I showed him my signature, his face lit up like a kid on Christmas morning. Who cared how much trouble this would be? We were going to married forever.

On June 19, we were on a plane to Washington so I could show off my groom to my family. We were also there for my granddaughter's high school/college graduation. While we were home, I drove him down the Washington side of the Columbia River to Long Beach. I showed him my dad's old house and the Long Beach Tavern, where my parents hung out. We crossed the Columbia River on the four-mile long Astoria Bridge and headed down the coast on the famed Highway 101. We visited Canyon Beach, where we saw Haystack Rock. If you have watched *The Goonies*, you have seen it too. We walked all around the town, visiting all the quaint little shops and stopped for ice cream. We headed back to Kelli's house, driving up the Oregon side of the Columbia River. Both sides have incredible views of the Columbia River, and just the vastness of greenery is stunning. I've always said the Northwest was so beautiful because God waters it daily. I was having so much fun showing Dick where I grew up and all my favorite places. Two years later, Kelli told me that when she asked him how he liked it, he responded with, "I might need a drink after putting up with your mother's driving." Kelli was surprised he didn't comment on sharing his new bride's childhood home, her memories, or the beauty of it all. Maybe she should have told me that then. But being the most supportive daughter that she is, she kept that to herself.

On July 9, we headed to Buffalo, New York. It was time for him to show off his bride. His family threw us a wedding reception, complete with the wedding cake, of which we smeared on each other's face and sealed it with a kiss. He took me to see Niagara Falls from the Canadian side. We had a beautiful dinner at the Queen Victoria Restaurant. The waiter got an extra tip by making sure we had a table by the rail, with a view of the US and Canadian falls. We listened to live music and watched fireworks. Did you know that they do a light show on the falls every night? Just wow! The next day, we took a trolley ride, visited an aquarium, and a fun little zoo. The little girl in me just can't get enough of that stuff.

We flew back to Colorado, and by the twenty-sixth, we were at Fiddler's Green Stadium in Denver, sitting in the VIP tent, watching Jason Aldean. Oh my, Dick even told me not to expect this every time because it was very expensive. Knowing Dick, I would never see this again. We were spitting distance from the stage and got a preconcert performance. The music was amazing, and then we went to the main stage for the real concert. There was food and booze—it was so fun!

In August, we started the kitchen remodel. I got to pick out all the cabinets and appliances, to include a new gas stove and an Instant Hot. I was feeling very spoiled. Our friends helped tear out the kitchen, and Casey came over from Idaho and tore up the tile floor and put up all the cabinets and the trim on. My kitchen turned out so totally amazing. We took a break to go to the Coors Field Stadium in Denver to watch my favorite band, Zac Brown. Labor-day weekend, we took his fifth wheel to Buena Vista, to the Seven Peaks Festival. Three days of country western artists playing on three stages, put on by another favorite, Dierks Bentley. I was feeling so spoiled by this new husband of mine and so grateful he was a concert junkie. I was so in love with my forever husband.

We were invited to Telluride in September for a wedding for his previous next-door neighbor's daughter. We were there for four days and spent most of that time in bed. This was the honeymoon we hadn't gotten. This husband at least matched my sex drive. That never was an issue.

October took us to Las Vegas for a HempWorx convention. We stayed at the famous Mirage Hotel. When we weren't attending convention stuff, we were hanging at the pool, drinking expensive tall drinks and soaking up sunshine. We were there for Dick's birthday, so I bought him Eagles' concert tickets. They were so very expensive, but so worth the look on his face when I gave them to him. He was so surprised. We did have so much fun!

October also brought another event, my appointment with Dr. Bob. He specialized in hormone replacement and memory care. Once he saw that my mother had Alzheimer's, he tested me. My new diagnosis was mild cognitive impairment with moderate risk for Alzheimer's. I had been having difficulties finding words and remembering some things. He put me on Aricept, which is prescribed for dementia and Alzheimer's. Now it was all hitting home that I, most likely, was heading down the same path as my mother. As my tears fell down my face, Dick made me laugh by telling me he'd buy a shock collar for me if I started to wander. He also said he would always take care of me. Too bad that would be stripped away from me too.

Casey, my forty-one-year-old carpenter son, moved from Idaho to Colorado Springs in the early fall of 2019; by November, he was living with us. I hadn't had a relationship with him for thirteen years because of his selfish ex-wife. I was so happy he was there. Dick was an introvert and had withdrawn into his phone, and I was lonely. When I would bring up the need for better communication in our marriage, he would tell me, "My ex-wife said the same thing."

Casey and I are both talkative, happy, positive, and fun. I was in heaven. I had someone to talk to. On most weekends, his sweet fiancé, Karen, would come to stay. I hadn't had family around for so long; this was amazing. It was really nice to not have to cook dinner seven nights a week. They liked to go in the kitchen together to create the most wonderful meals. Dick never cooked, and sometimes,

I felt like the mother bird feeding her young three times a day.

Dick's son, Alan, who was twenty-nine, living in the basement, rarely came upstairs and was extremely lazy in my book. I had worked full-time and went to nursing school full-time while raising four kids to get my degree. This young man only went to school, most of it online, worked a few weekend shifts at the local liquor store, and gamed on his big-screen TV. He had the whole basement to himself—with two bedrooms, full bathroom, and living room with fireplace. He had the old fridge and microwave from the upstairs-kitchen remodel too. Even the washer and dryer were down there. And he paid no rent. And he did no work on the property. I think Dick and his ex-wife suffered from divorce guilt because neither of them could stop treating Alan like he was still twelve.

Casey didn't pay rent either; the difference was, Casey had a bedroom upstairs and everything else was shared space with us. He also worked for us on the property. He helped remodel our kitchen, hung all the cabinets, installed lights, and installed the new toilet. While we were in Texas from January through April 2020, Casey would put up new lights in the hallway, install a new double shower head in the bathroom at his expense, fix my soap dispenser in my new farm sink, clean out the garage, built Dick a new workbench as a welcome home gift, and Karen would clean the house on a regular basis.

Casey had built some trusses for a customer who decided not to take them. Casey offered them to Dick for $1200. Casey delivered them, and then Dick told me he'll only pay $1000. I said, "So you're going to cheat Casey out of $200 for his labor?" He didn't say anything. I paid the two-hundred-dollar difference. Cheap ass!

November came, and we had a wonderful big family Thanksgiving dinner on the beautiful huge table Casey had made and sold to us. I was in love with having family to entertain. Dick's oldest son, daughter-in-law, and their three precious young kiddos lived very close to us. Christmas was fabulous too. We had our Christmas on the twenty-second so we could leave for Texas a few days later. This Snowbird life was going to be our future.

The first time I saw Dick's evil side was when we first got back to Texas in January 2020. We got in a fight over money, and he shouted at me, "Why don't you just have your son bring your RV down here?"

I said, "Well, that's great, except it's snowed in on YOUR property!" Over the next year, Dick's evil side would come out more and more. I didn't understand it. I still don't. How could my knight in shining armor, who supposedly adored and loved me, be mean and uncaring to me?

We spent January and February in New Braunfels and then headed to South Padre Island for the next two months. Our friends brought their camper down too. And then COVID hit. By the end of March, toilet paper and cleaning supplies became quite the commodity. One time, I couldn't find eggs for two weeks. By April, it had gotten pretty weird. The beach would be empty. We were told you could only be outside for exercise. One time, we were riding our electric bikes, when the beach patrol pulled Dick over to tell him he had to pedal, or it wasn't exercise. Oh, brother! When the killer mosquitoes moved in mid-month, I was ready to go home. If I was going to be locked down, I wanted to be on our property with family.

Dick and his friend co-owned a pontoon boat and a little ski boat. They were moored at Pueblo Reservoir. It was really nice having them always in the water, making it really convenient to go down and play on the water. There was an RV park there too. Between camping, playing on the water, and backyard BBQs, it was a pretty good summer. We even got some work done outside. Casey built a sweet little greenhouse for us, and I even threw a greenhouse potluck party, with lots of family and friends. A cornhole tournament happened too. I love to entertain, and I was certainly in my element.

One of our summer projects was a retaining wall. Casey connected Dick to his landscaping buddies and got him a smoking deal on boulders and the huge excavator with the operator to place them. Casey and Dick even built an oversized carport next to the garage. It was all done, except putting shingles on the roof. Off to the lake we went camping.

Dick, me, Casey, Karen, and Casey's daughter, Susie, who was seven, all went camping at Pueblo Reservoir that weekend. Susie had already spent six weeks living with us for Casey's summer visitation; it was only supposed to be four. She was a very difficult spoiled only child, so by the beginning of August, all our nerves were frayed. On Monday, Casey, Karen, and Susie left to go home. We would spend another night, and finally, we were alone.

The next morning, August 4, Casey called me to vent. After just a few words, he asked me to take him off speakerphone. So I did and went up into the bedroom to talk to him. The night before, he had brought Susie home to Alan throwing a wild party with his friends. The music was loud and totally inappropriate for a seven-year-old. Casey asked Alan if he could turn it down and change the music. Of which Alan said no. Casey ended up taking Susie to bed with him; she normally slept on the couch; he wasn't happy about that. Then when morning came, he got up to find the kitchen a total mess. Here we go again. Alan liked to cook, but he sure could destroy a kitchen. Dick and I's first fight had been about Alan using my brand-new stove, before I even got to, and leaving it a disaster with fried greasy hamburger everywhere, dishes all over the counters, and garbage on the floor. Dick always took Alan's side. I never was first in our marriage. When I asked if he'd seen the kitchen, he got angry at me. Said it doesn't matter, and Alan said he'd clean it up that morning.

I said, "Who lets it get like that in the first place?"

He said, "I don't know if this is going to work." I wish I would have agreed with him instead of arguing that he wasn't getting out of this marriage that easy.

The morning Casey called me to vent, we were still camping at the Reservoir but were slated to go home that day. When I got off the phone, Dick asked me what that was all about. I told him, and my expectation was that he would say he'd talk to Alan when we got home. I might have even expected him to say, "Casey and Karen need to move out. We'll talk about it with them when we get home." But that isn't what happened.

Dick took his phone outside and called Casey. He yelled at him to "get the f———k off his property and all his f———king shit too." Soon my phone rang with Casey telling me what Dick had just done. And he had yelled all that while Casey was driving with Susie in the truck, which means it all came over the speakerphone. Casey asked Dick to just stop, that Susie was in the truck. Dick responded he didn't care; he was sure she had heard it all before. I couldn't believe it. Who does that to their wife's family? Without us even talking about it! When I asked Dick why he did that, he said he was sick of Casey tattling on Alan. Divorce guilt 101.

By the time we got home that day, Casey and his friend, Brian, were hooking up his boat and work trailer to their trucks to start the move-out process.

At this point, I asked Dick, "So am I supposed to move out too?"

He said, "Probably so."

I said, "But this is my home too."

He said, "This isn't your home, and it never will be!"

My heart shattered into a million pieces. Once again, I would be moving out of a home I had decorated and poured my love into, making it my forever home. I was so mad I was back in these shoes again!

Casey and Karen continued to come and get loads of Casey's stuff over the next week, but Dick always had to get in Casey's face, bullying him. He couldn't just sit in his chair and let my son move off his property. I would sit on the porch crying as Casey and Karen drove away, and Dick wouldn't say a word. So much for caring about your wife's feelings.

Dick lies! A few days after Casey had started moving out, I couldn't find my phone, so I asked Dick if he had seen it.

He said, "No."

I asked him, "Could you call my phone so I can find it?"

It was in the bathroom, but when I picked it up, there was a message from Casey, "Mom, did you send me this message?" I scrolled up to read the text Dick had sent: "Mean and stupid. Did you even talk to Alan last night? Passive-aggressive… You're just as bad. Just cry to your momma, honey. Poor Casey. The kid just can't get a break. Blah, blah, blah." I was furious. I said to Dick, "You lied to me. You not only knew where my phone was, but you used MY phone to send MY son a mean ugly text." He looked at me with the most evil, ugly sneer on his face and said, "Oh, honey, everybody lies." The hair stood up on my arms.

I spent the next few days cleaning my RV and replacing all the things I had moved to his RV, and added all my stuff from the house to live in it again. I couldn't move out yet because Gracie, our pup, had an appointment to get spayed, and I wanted her to come home to a home she knew after surgery. I spent the first couple of nights in the spare bedroom, but I couldn't stand knowing he was in the next bedroom and was too stubborn to come and get me. The remainder of the nights, I took the girls (two dogs) and slept in the RV. On August 12, I drove Guppy (my

RV) down to a park in Colorado Springs. Dick never called to see if I arrived safely or had any trouble hooking up.

When Casey got off work, he picked me up to take me up to the house to pick up my truck. He asked me if I minded helping him finish loading the rest of his stuff. I said, "Sure." When we arrived, Dick was eager for us to get loaded. He even brought Casey's crates up from the barn. At one point, Casey asked me to go get his computer off the desk and don't forget the cables as those were his. I disconnected everything except the printer that was Dick's and the little white box next to it that I assumed was the router. I put everything in the back seat of Casey's truck.

It was at the end of our loading that Casey went to take the drawers out of the desk. Dick told him he had bought that desk from him. Casey said, "No, Dick, I gave this desk to my mom." It was then that I walked in and hearing their argument, I said, "Dick, you're wrong. Casey sold you the table he made for $3,500, but the desk was a gift to me from my son." Dick continued to argue. Casey kept saying, "Dick, look, this isn't necessary. You asked me to move out, and I'm doing that. I just want to get the rest of my stuff and the money you owe me for the carport and go." Dick said he wasn't going to pay Casey because he hadn't finished the job by putting the shingles on. Casey said, "Okay, instead of $1,000, just pay me $750, and we're even." Dick never did pay Casey.

I went out to put something in my truck that was under the carport, next to the garage, when I heard a commotion in the garage. I darted into the garage to see Dick turn toward me, hands up with blood on them, blood on his lip, looking up at the camera, and back to me saying, "Honey, I'm not a fighter." I could see his lip was split. I said, "Are you kidding me? You have poked and prodded this young man for eight days, calling him every name in the book. You got what you deserved." I never did see Casey hit Dick. Dick ran into the bathroom and locked the door. When he came out, Casey was yelling at him, "I'm tired of you and that piece of shit in the basement being disrespectful to my mother for over a year." I actually was proud of him for sticking up for his mom. We ended up in the living room, where I was between Casey and Dick, facing Casey, saying, "Let's just go." There were lots of heated arguing, and finally we left.

What next? Well, Dick called the sheriff, lodged a complaint against Casey, and went to the ER. Once there, he checked in on Facebook, not saying why he was there, but that he was sad. He had eighty-seven comments from well-wishing friends. I believe he did this to document he was at the ER. Once in the ER, they did every CT and X-ray available. All tests were negative. No fractures to his nose or jaw, no broken ribs, and no lost teeth. Dick later told me that Casey had hit him eighteen to twenty times. This was just not possible. I saw Casey's hand an hour after the incident, it was slightly swollen, but he was able to bend all his fingers, no broken bones. I handed him some ice. He went to work the next day. He's a carpenter, and this was his dominant hand. Certainly not the hand you would see if he had hit someone's head eighteen to twenty times! More lies!

Dick also sent me this text on the fifteenth: "Someone unscrewed the cable from the back of the infinity router box that you brought back to the house the other day. You had to intentionally unscrew the cable to disconnect it. Once that was done, the Wi-Fi was down and so were the cameras. You both knew that. Was my beating premeditated? Was I going to get my ass kicked no matter what I did or said? Keep in mind, Dick outweighs Casey by one hundred pounds, and Casey is not a boy; he is a forty-one-year old man.

It was after I had moved to the RV park that Casey and Karen told me of an event that had happened to them during the summer, involving the gifted cowboy. Casey and Karen were at the antique mall when a middle-aged man in a cowboy hat came up to Karen, who was singing, and told her that her voice was beautiful. Casey was a few tables away and looked up to see Karen talking to this man. He didn't worry about it because Karen talks to everyone. So when Casey got up there to them, Karen said to Casey, "You need to hear what this man has to say."

The man introduced himself to Casey and said, "You guys are a great couple, you've both been through a lot, and you will be together forever, but I want to talk to you about your mother. She is very successful, isn't she?"

Casey said, "Yes, she is."

He then said, "But it's her professional life that is very successful. Her personal life, maybe not so much, right?"

Casey said, "Yes, that's true."

And then he said, "The man that she's with is very evil. He's an alien, and he's using her. And you live with her, don't you?"

Casey said, "Yes."

Then he said, "You have to get out. This will not end well for you."

Later, Casey surely regretted he hadn't taken the gifted cowboy's advice. Once again, the hair stood up on my arms.

August 28, I filed the divorce papers. If you don't want the military wife, you don't get to keep the military benefits. Dick never put my name on any of his accounts or life insurance policies and, in fact, had me sign a prenup the day before we were married. I asked for a copy of it when I filed the divorce; he said he didn't know where it was. Another lie. It was never notarized, and I think he was trying to figure out how to get the return of my wedding ring in there somehow. He never did give me a copy. I never did know how much money or assets he really had. He did tell me some of his friends had asked him if this was a mother-son scam job. Are you kidding me?

A few weeks later, Dick sent me a copy of the report he filed with Tricare. They had paid all of it but $153, but noted that if this was an assault, they could go after the person for the bill. Dick filled this out with Casey's phone number, date of birth, and the case number. He was dead set on revenge against Casey.

I moved back to Texas September 29 and, once again, lived in my RV. Dick's mother died on the second, and Dick asked me to go to New York with him for the funeral. We were there nine days, and it felt like we were getting back together. So when he came to Texas the end of October, I thought he had dropped the charges against Casey and was focused on putting our marriage back together. I stopped the divorce.

Much later in December, I ran across that ER bill that still had not been paid. When I asked Dick why he didn't pay it, he said, "I did pay it." So I called them the next day. No it wasn't paid, so I paid it. Dick lied! Later, he transferred $155 into my checking, and when I asked what that was for, he replied, "For the erroneous UCHealth bill you paid. This all needs to come back on him!" And then there were the text messages between Dick and Detective William on Dick's phone. They were from September, October, November, and December, while he was sleeping in my bed! I truly believe if he wanted this marriage to heal and survive, he would have dropped it, but he was hell-bent on destroying my son. Neither Casey nor I knew why. Casey really liked Dick. This was perhaps the first time a father figure had taken interest in him. Dick would even go to Casey's work sites to see how to build things and to help him. They were building a relationship. Until this event happened.

No charges had been filed until November; the fight was in August. Dick had continuously pushed for "felony-assault-with-a-deadly-weapon" charges until he got them. Deadly weapon, you ask? Dick lied and said Casey threw a cordless drill at him, hitting him in the back. Nope, that didn't happen either. I was livid, and for a second time, I filed for a divorce. Did he really think he could destroy my son and keep the wife? I kicked him out, and he went back home to Colorado.

Sounds like the end, right? Not so fast. Casey was arrested December 29. He had to pay $1,100 for bail and $8,000 for an attorney. For eight months, my son lived with the threat that he could go to prison for ten to twenty years, not to mention the $9,100 debt he now owed and possibly the $12,000 medical bill from Tricare on top of that. I am grateful that Casey and Karen's relationship survived this ordeal.

Dick finally agreed to go to mediation. There Dick asked for probation, anger management classes, two hundred and forty community service hours, compensation and a letter to his mother, with a copy to him. When the mediator asked Casey what he wanted from Dick, he replied, "A hug." I am so proud of the son I raised. What did Dick get? A certified copy of the letter Casey wrote to his mother. As for compensation, the mediator said it was a wash for the money Dick owed Casey. Maybe now, we all can move on with our lives and put this horrible nightmare behind us.

So how do I really feel about this TENTH marriage ending in divorce? Well, just like the rest, hindsight will always be twenty-twenty. Maybe if Dick had been more concerned about his relationship with his new wife than sticking up for Alan and being so focused on money, I would not be living in an RV. I often wonder how different our marriage would have been had Alan moved out when Dick brought his new wife home, and Casey hadn't moved in. What would our life have looked like if it had just been Dick and I in it? I think there were lots of reasons this marriage broke down, but I also believe they could have all been handled had he put me first, talked to me, and NEVER lied to me. We should have been one unit that kids and money couldn't break. Sad, just so sad!

Who knows where I go from here! Two years from when my knight in shining armor arrived in Texas to scoop me off my feet, here I am, single and living in my RV again, almost like those two years never happened. The good memories were very good—the places we went, the concerts we attended, the camping, the happy hours with friends, and the work we did on his beautiful property. This whole thing is just heartbreaking. I wish him all the best. I just can't be with someone who lies to me and doesn't think twice about hurting my family. This marriage had a wonderful beginning and a horrible ending!

All the closure I need is knowing I am better than that, and I deserve so much more. I'd like to think my rose-colored glasses are finally smashed to smithereens, but if there is one thing I know about me, it's that I am a total romantic at heart.

Thank you for letting me share my life with you. The divorce is final, and I moved into a beautiful apartment across from the pool. I go to Pilates every day I can and take my pups to the dog park often. I have a large group of women, here in this community, that surround me with love and support. If you don't have a good support system, get one. My girlfriends are beyond priceless.

Writing this book has been very therapeutic for me. I would not change a thing in my past because it has made me who I am today. I am one strong, resilient, tenacious, optimistic, positive, God-loving, beautiful lady—at sixty-three! After all of this, I am still looking for my ONE and to fall head over heels in love. Life is so incredibly GOOD! I cannot wait for the next adventure to begin. What will your adventure look like?

About the Author

Jan Kelsey is from the Northwest but is most at home in New Braunfels, Texas. The military brought her here, but the beauty of the Hill Country and all her loving, supporting girlfriends kept her here. Her days are spent with a trip to Pilates and several trips to the dog park with her companions, Gracie the mini Goldendoodle and Tilly the six-pound Poodle. Precious girlfriend time is usually spent over a glass of wine at her favorite winery, Water2Wine.

Jan's daughter, Kelli, had been asking her for ten years to write a book, often saying, "Mom, nobody can make this shit up!" After the last catastrophe, it was finally time to tell her story. Jan lives by a saying that hangs on her wall: **Courage does not always roar. Sometimes, it is the quiet voice at the end of the day, saying, "I will try again tomorrow."** The adventures ahead are just beginning, and Jan couldn't be more excited about what the future holds. Maybe even a second book, who knows.